Programming for
Absolute Beginners

Programming for Absolute Beginners

Mark Lassoff

LearnToProgram, Inc.
Vernon, Connecticut

LearnToProgram.tv, Incorporated
27 Hartford Turnpike Suite 206
Vernon, CT06066
contact@learntoprogram.tv
(860) 840-7090

©2014 by LearnToProgram.tv, Incorporated

ISBN-10: 0990402037
ISBN-13: 978-0-9904020-3-9

Mark Lassoff, Writer, Publisher
Kevin Hernandez, VP/ Production
Alison Downs, Copy Editor
Alexandria O'Brien, Book Layout

Dedication

To REO Speedwagon, Journey, and Styx who provided the soundtrack for this project.

Courses Available from LearnToProgram, Inc.

3D Fundamentals with iOS
Advanced Javascript Development
AJAX Development
Android Development for Beginners
Become a Certified Web Developer (Level 1)
Become a Certified Web Developer (Level 2)
C Programming for Beginners
C++ for Beginners
Construct 2 for Beginners
Creating a PHP Login Script
CSS Development (with CSS3!)
Design for Coders
Famu.os Javascript Framework
Game Development Fundamentals with Python
Game Development with Python
GitHub Fundamentals
HTML and CSS for Beginners (with HTML5)
HTML5 Mobile App Development with PhoneGap
Introduction to Web Development
iOS Development Code Camp
iOS Development for Beginners Featuring iOS6/7
Java Programming for Beginners
Javascript for Beginners
Joomla for Beginners
jQuery for Beginners
Mobile Game Development with iOS
Node.js for Beginners
Objective C for Beginners
Photoshop for Coders
PHP & MySQL for Beginners
Programming for Absolute Beginners
Project Management with Microsoft Project
Python for Beginners
Ruby on Rails for Beginners
SQL Database for Beginners
User Experience Design

Books from LearnToProgram, Inc.

Create Your Own MP3 Player with HTML5
CSS Development (with CSS3!)
Game Development with Python
HTML and CSS for Beginners
Javascript for Beginners
PHP and MySQL for Beginners
Programming for Absolute Beginners
Python for Beginners
SQL Database for Beginners
Swift Fundamentals: The Language of iOS Development

TABLE OF CONTENTS

About the Author:

Mark Lassoff

Mark Lassoff's parents frequently claim that Mark was born to be a programmer. In the mid-eighties when the neighborhood kids were outside playing kickball and throwing snowballs, Mark was hard at work on his Commodore 64 writing games in the BASIC programming language. Computers and programming continued to be a strong interest in college where Mark majored in communication and computer science. Upon completing his college career, Mark worked in the software and web development departments at several large corporations.

In 2001, on a whim, while his contemporaries were conquering the dot com world, Mark accepted a position training programmers in a technical training center in Austin, Texas. It was there that he fell in love with teaching programming.

Teaching programming has been Mark's passion for the last 10 years. Today, Mark is a top technical trainer, traveling the country providing leading courses for software and web developers. Mark's training clients include the Department of Defense, Lockheed Martin, Discover Card Services, and Kaiser Permanente. In addition to traditional classroom training, Mark releases courses on the web, which have been taken by programming students all over the world.

He lives near Hartford, Connecticut where he is in the process of redecorating his condominium.

About the Course Producer:

Kevin Hernandez

Kevin has worked at LearnToProgram since the company's formation in 2011. Kevin is responsible for the entire production process including video editing, distribution and testing of lab exercises. Kevin plays the French horn in multiple bands and orchestras throughout Connecticut.

CHAPTER 1

WRITING YOUR FIRST PROGRAM

Welcome! If this is your first time programming, congratulations! You're about to start an adventure that most find very rewarding. If you are trying to learn after a previous abortive attempt, you deserve recognition as well. Tackling programming isn't always easy — but it's not outside the grasp of the average person, either.

Over the years, I've taught programming to over 100,000 people both online and in person. The programmers I've met over the years — both beginners and seasoned vets — have come from a variety of backgrounds. I've found that both PhDs and high school dropouts can make good programmers. I've had mathematicians, psychiatrists, and 12 year-olds in my classes over the years and all have been able to learn some programming.

You will learn, too. In this introductory chapter — which is specially designed for the slightly apprehensive beginner — I am going to take you step-by-step through the process of writing your first program. You don't need any special equipment except a laptop or desktop computer. (If you're brave, you can use an iPad...but it wouldn't be my first choice.)

So without further delay, let's get started!

WHAT YOU'RE GOING TO LEARN

This first chapter will serve as an introduction on how to set up your programming environment and get started. Each chapter following is designed to take you through the basics of a certain aspect of development and give you a foundation for greater learning. Just to give you some context, here's what's coming up in the rest of the book:

Chapter 2: Input and Output
Input and output are key to any program. In this chapter we'll look at how to get data into and out of a program.

Chapter 3: Understanding Variables
Variables are key building blocks in any program. This chapter takes readers through declaring and utilizing variables in expressions.

Chapter 4: Conditionals and Loops
Conditionals and Loops are structures which allow programs to make decisions that alter the execution of the program and result. These will be demonstrated and explained in this chapter.

Chapter 5: Dealing with Data
Almost every useful program, to some extent, deals with data. In this chapter you'll learn how to store various forms of data in a program.

Chapter 6: Putting it All Together
In this final chapter of the book, readers will learn how to create a useful program that processes and stores data, using the skills developed in the previous chapters.

Before we write any programs, we have to get your development environment set up. I won't make you buy anything (with the exception of one $2.99 program, if you want to run this all on an iPad), and you may even have a few options to choose from.

Figure 1.1: The Author's Development Environment. Doobie Brothers' music not included.

SETTING UP YOUR DEVELOPMENT ENVIRONMENT

ON THE MAC

If you're using a Mac you have very little set up to do. We're going to be using a language called Python in this book and it runs natively in the Mac's command line. If you've never used the command line before, it's pretty easy to find. Look inside your applications folder and find the utilities folder. Inside the utilities folder you'll find the "Terminal" program. Double-click it.

This Book Uses

Python

Programming Language

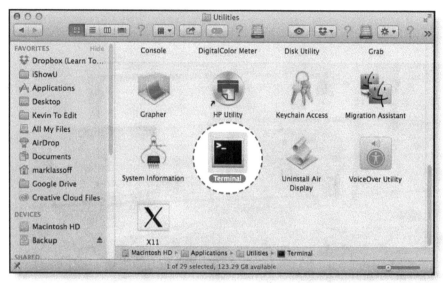

Figure 1.2: The Utilities folder on the Mac

When you double-click, after a moment, the terminal program will load and the command line will display. The cursor will appear flashing at the end of a line known as the prompt.

Figure 1.3: The terminal in the author's computer. Note that the author changed the default colors through the terminal's preferences.

ON THE PC

The PC command line does not process Python code out-of-the-box like the Mac. I recommend you use the virtual Linux server provided by my friends at Koding.com. Point your browser to www.Koding.com and register for their free account. The free account gives you a virtual Linux machine that you can access through your web browser — and it can process Python code identically to the Mac.

Once you have your account, click the green button toward the upper left-hand corner of the screen that looks similar to a DOS prompt. That will put you in the command line of your terminal.

Figure 1.4 Command Line in Koding.com. You can using Koding.com on a Mac as well if that is your preference.

ON THE IPAD (IF YOU DARE)

I wanted to include this option for the tablet-centric. I should note that I haven't actually tried coding on the iPad myself, but I imagine it will work just fine. In the App Store you'll find Python 2.7 by Jonathan Hosmer. This is a full Python development environment for Python programming.

iPad

If you elect this option, download the app and read whatever documentation is included. The process for executing code will likely be different since we are working in a command line environment, however the code will be identical.

Figure 1.5: Python on iOS requires this $2.99 download through iTunes

If you do get all this working on the iPad, I would like to hear from you. Let me know your thoughts on using this environment and on coding on a tablet in general.

WRITING AND RUNNING YOUR CODE

Now that you have your environment set up, it's time to (finally) write some code. We'll write code in a text editor. A text editor is different than a word processor. A word processor will introduce invisible formatting code into a file. If you were to run code written in a word processor it would likely error due to the embedded formatting code.

A text editor, on the other hand, saves the text you enter as pure text — without introducing any unnecessary formatting. The text produced by a text editor can be easily processed by the Python interpreter. Within the command line environments in the Koding.com virtual machine and on the Mac there are two text editors you can use. They are known as nano and vi. These text editors have a heritage that goes back to the 1970s — so as you use them you can truly feel "old school!"

NANO

Nano is an easy to use Linux-based editor. It's pretty intuitive. You can simply start typing your code when the nano environment loads. Nano has a number of control codes which are listed at the bottom of your screen for your reference. The most important to note are CTRL-O which saves your file and CTRL-X which exits nano and returns you to the command line.

By default, nano will save your file in the same folder you were in when you opened nano itself.

> You can start nano by typing **nano** and then enter on the command line.

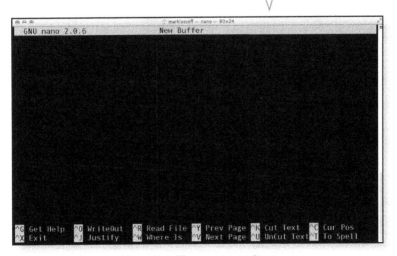

Figure 1.6: The nano text editor.

VI

vi is a slightly more complex (and even more "old school") text editor. The most important thing to understand about vi is that there are two modes: command mode and insert mode. To move into insert mode, press 'i' on your keyboard. When you want to move into command mode to issue commands like write and quit, hit the ESC key. If you screw up and find yourself in the wrong mode, press ESC a lot and that seems to get you back into command mode from wherever you are at.

There's an old joke about vi that goes like this: vi has two modes, and you're in the wrong one. (If you don't think it's funny now, you will after you use vi for a bit!)

When you enter vi, type i to move into insert mode and you'll be able to type your code. When you're done, hit ESC to move into command mode. All commands must be preceded by a colon. So to write your file you'll enter :w. To quit you'll enter :q. vi also lets you combine commands. For example, the combination :wq will write your file and then quit back to the command line.

> You can start vi by typing **vi** and then return on the command line.

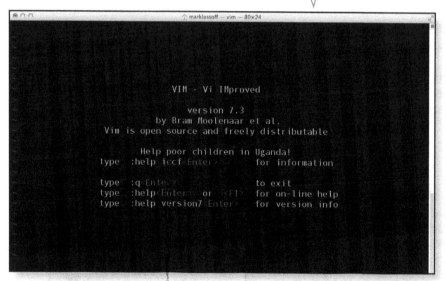

Figure 1.7: vi wants you to help poor children in Uganda. It offers limited help for new programmers worldwide.

You can start vi by typing vi and then hitting return on the command line.

So now you should have your text editor started and be ready to enter your code. Enter the following code into your text editor exactly as it appears:

```
print "Hello World."
print "This is my first program.  Programmers
are rock stars!"
```

It should be at least somewhat evident what this code does. The **print** command prints content to the command line. In this case you are printing two strings. Strings are simply lines of characters. Strings are always enclosed in quotes.

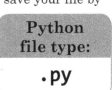

Once you've typed the code, it's time to run it. In nano, save your file by typing CTRL-W. When prompted, enter the filename HelloWorld.py. The ".py" extension indicates that this is a Python source code file. Next enter CTRL-X to quit and you'll be returned to the command line. In vi, enter command mode and then save your file by typing :w HelloWorld.py. This will write your file under the appropriate file name.

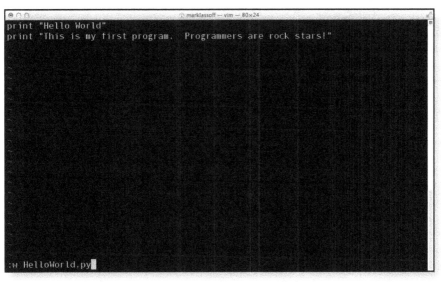

Figure 1.8: Saving your file in vi.

Finally, in vi, hit :q to quit and return to the command line.

Now your cursor should appear at the prompt. Run the program by entering the following at the prompt (don't type the '$'— that just represents the prompt itself):

```
$ python HelloWorld.py
```

If you've done everything correctly, you should see the result of your program printed before the next prompt.

```
●○○                          ⭕ marklassoff — bash — 80×24
Marks-MacBook-Pro-3:~ marklassoff$ python HelloWorld.py
Hello World
This is my first program.  Programmers are rock stars!
Marks-MacBook-Pro-3:~ marklassoff$
```

Figure 1.9: Execution of the HelloWorld.py program

If your output doesn't look similar to *figure 1.9*, you need to load your text editor and code again and find your error. You can reload your code at the command line prompt with the following command:

vi:
```
vi HelloWorld.py
```

nano:
```
nano HelloWorld.py
```

Congratulations! You have successfully written your first program.

UNDERSTANDING THE PRINT COMMAND

In the preceding example we used the print command to print out a string. The print command is also capable of printing out the following:

Integers: Integers are "whole numbers" and don't have a decimal point. In Python, you can print an integer like this:

```
print 2573
```

Floating Point Numbers: Floats are more precise numbers that include a decimal point. In Python you can print a floating point number like this:

```
print 3.45783
```

Expressions: Expressions must be evaluated before a result is determined. Expressions are usually arithmetic problems. To print an expression in Python:

```
print 3.0/(6+4)
```

In the expression above, the part of the expression in parenthesis will be evaluated first due to the order of operations. The result printed would be 0.3.

We'll look at expressions more closely in our next chapter.

NANO COMMANDS TO NOTE	
Command Function:	**Shortcut:**
Save File (WriteOut)	CTRL-O
Exit	CTRL-X
Get Help	CTRL-G
Justify - reflow the text	CTRL-J
Read File	CTRL-R
Find/Search (Where Is)	CTRL-W
Previous/Next Page	CTRL-Y / CTRL-V
Copy/Paste Text (Cut/Uncut)	CTRL-K / CTRL-U
Show Line Number/Info (Current Position)	CTRL-C
Spell Check (To Spell)	CTRL-T

VI COMMANDS TO NOTE	
Command Function:	**Shortcut:**
Change Mode (Command Mode)	ESC
Insert (text) Mode	i
Write File	:w
Quit	:q
Write File and Quit (combined commands)	:wq
Undo One Step	u
Delete Single Character	x
Delete Entire Line	dd
Copy Current Line (yank, cut)	yy
Paste	p

CHAPTER 2

INPUT AND OUTPUT

In this chapter we're going to look more closely at input and output, which are, perhaps, the two most critical concepts in any program. In the previous chapter we looked closely at the output that can be produced with the **print** command. With **print** we were able to output three types of data to the command line screen: strings, integers and floating point numbers. The programs we wrote, however, have no capacity to take input and process data. In this chapter we're going to look closely at two types of input. Input statements will allow us to programmatically request input from the user. We'll then use command line parameters to provide inputs to our program.

As we look at output, we'll also look at directing our output to a file instead of back to the command line.

 So now it's time to put on your favorite programming music (I suggest The Cure), open your **nano** or **vi** text editor and start coding...

INPUT STATEMENTS

We're going to start with a program that calculates the area of a rectangle based on the length of a *sideA* input and a *sideB* input. Let's start with the code. Key the following Python Code into your text editor:

```
print "RECTANGLE AREA CALCULATOR"
sideA = input("What is the length of sideA? " )
sideB = input("What is the length of sideB? " )
area = sideA * sideB
print "The area of your rectangle is", area
```

Once you are sure you have keyed in the program correctly, go ahead and run the program on the command line. I saved mine as **square.py**. Your output should look similar to *figure 2.1*.

Figure 2.1: Execution of the square.py program which takes input from the user via the Python **input()** function.

Based on context and the program execution, you've probably already guessed what the **input()** function does. Let's break it down:

input()

```
age = input("How old are you?")
```

In the example above, whatever the user types at the prompt *"How old are you?"* is going to be assigned to the variable **age**. We're going to take a closer look at variables in the next chapter – for right now, just consider variables a temporary storage place for values. These values can be strings, floats, or integers.

Let's try a new example. Create a new file in your text editor called stringInput.py. You can do this in vi, for example, by typing the following command on the command line: **vi stringInput.py**.

Key in the following code:

```
name = input("What's your name?")
print "Hello, " , name
```

Exit your text editor and execute the program from your command line with the command **python stringInput.py**. The result may not be what you expect.

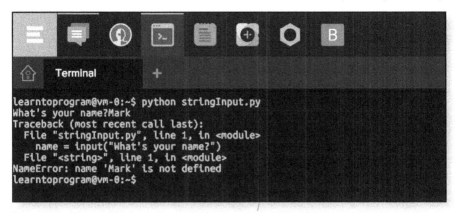

Figure 2.2: Uh-oh. This can't be good. My name isn't defined? Disturbing.

So what happened? Instead of running to completion, the program exited with an error. Luckily the error is easy to fix. The input() function automatically converts whatever data is entered into a floating point number or integer. When you enter an actual string, it causes the error you see in *figure 2.2*. We have another version of the input() function that is intended for string use. Edit your code as follows:

```
name = raw_input("What's your name?")
print "Hello, " , name
```

NOTE: For a few of you this may have worked fine. The reason is, you are using a different version of Python that permits string usage with the input() function.

Figure 2.3: So much better with raw_input()!

When you're working with strings, you should use the **raw_input()** function which does not attempt to convert the data entered into a number. It keeps the data "raw" just as entered by the user.

raw_input()

PARAMETERIZED INPUT

A second way in which input can be submitted into a Python program is through the command line when the program is run. This is done through command line arguments. Right now when you run your program in the command line, you type the **python** command followed by the filename of the program you're trying to run. However, if you include parameters, it would look more like this:

```
$ python moreInput.py arg1 arg2 arg3
```

In the example above, we still use the **python** command and the filename of the program we'd like to run, but we follow it with the arguments that will be the input in the program. For example, if we wanted a program to receive the users name and age as input, the parameters might look something like this:

```
$ python moreInput.py Mark 40
```

The values "Mark" and "40", which are separated by a single space, are passed to the program and can be used as input. Let's see how. Key in the following example and save it as **moreInput.py**:

```
import sys

print "Your name is ", sys.argv[1]
print "Your age is ", sys.argv[2]
print "All the arguments: " , sys.argv
```

Next, let's run the program and supply command line arguments as input:

```
$ python moreInput.py Mark 40
```

You should get a result similar to the one pictured in *figure 2.4:*

On the first line of this program, we encounter our first **import** statement. Imports are used in many languages to add an additional library of commands to the language that are not in the language core. In this case, we're adding the **sys** library which contains commands regarding the Python system itself. It has the necessary code commands that allow us to access the command line arguments.

import statement

> **NOTE:** The terms parameter and argument can be used interchangeably.

The arguments come into Python numbered sequentially, so in our case, the user's name is argument number one and the age is argument number two. In code, we call these **sys.argv[1]** and **sys.argv[2]** respectively. The last line of the program tells Python to output all of the command line parameters. If you study the screenshot carefully, you may notice something interesting–**sys.argv[1]** is *not* the first parameter.

The first parameter is the name of the file we're running with Python. This is **sys.argv[0]**. The name of the file that we run is actually an argument of the **Python** command that we issue. This is often a point of confusion when working with command line arguments in Python.

OUTPUT TO A FILESTREAM

Your output does not have to be directed back to the command line. It can be directed to a file for more permanent storage. Being able to store data (more or less) permanently is an important skill for programmers to learn. Let's write a program in which we ask the user to enter several pieces of data and we then store those in a file.

Key in the following code:

```
name = raw_input("What is your name? ")
email = raw_input("What is your email? ")
favoriteBand = raw_input("What is your favorite
band? ")
outputString = name + "|" + email + "|" +
favoriteBand
fileName = name + ".txt"

#open the file
file = open(fileName, "wb")
file.write(outputString)
print outputString , " is written to file " ,
fileName
file.close()
```

This is definitely the most complex program we've written yet. Go ahead and run it on the command line and make sure you don't get any errors. If everything runs correctly, your command line should look something like this:

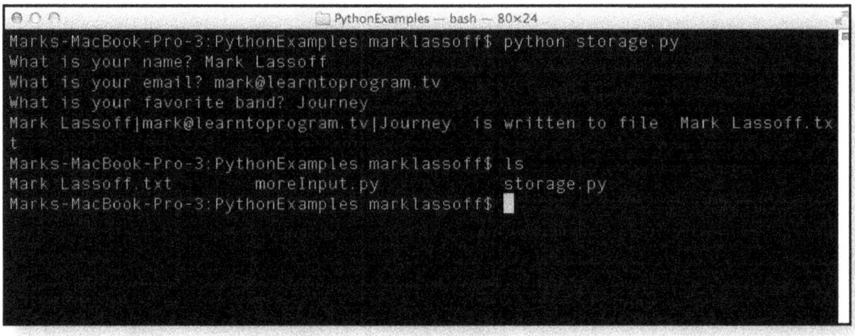

Figure 2.5: The program stored the data in a file called Mark Lassoff.txt which is now available in the directory listing by using the *ls* command on the command line.

While the code for this program is somewhat longer than what you are used to at this point, it is still fairly straightforward. When the program runs we prompt the user for their name, email, and name of their favorite band. We store that information in variables. We then create a new variable called **outputString** which contains the information the user typed and some formatting to make the information readable when stored.

The **fileName** variable is populated by user input and will be used to store the actual file output.

```
file = open(fileName, "wb")
file.write(outputString)
print outputString , " is written to file " ,
fileName
file.close()
```

The first line of this series opens a file, using the **fileName** created earlier. **wb** is the file mode which indicates that we are opening the file with permission to write to it. **file.write()** obviously writes the actual data to the file that has been opened. We then alert the user to what has occured and use **file.close()** to close the actual file that we've written.

file.write()   **file.close()**

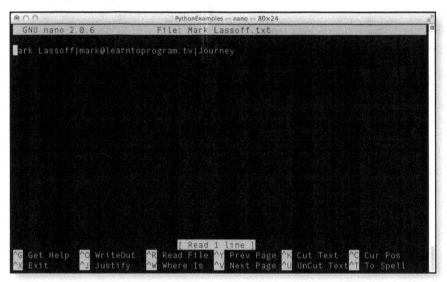

Figure 2.6 We opened "Mark Lassoff.txt" in the text editor and you can see the data that has been written to the disk.

Congratulations! You've written a program that stores data permanently as output. You are well on your way to being a programmer!

CHAPTER 3

UNDERSTANDING VARIABLES

In the previous chapter, we looked at input and output, which allow us to get data into and out of our Python program. In this lesson we'll take a closer look at one of the most important aspects of programming—variables. You may not equate variables with computer programming, but you've likely been using variables since high school if you took courses in Algebra, Chemistry, and Physics. In classic "solve for x" problems, x is a variable.

Let's first take a look at how the Python programming environment handles variables.

DECLARING AND INITIALIZING VARIABLES

Many languages require that you declare a variable before use—however, in Python we have a simpler paradigm that allows variables to be declared and initialized at the same time. In Python, variables aren't differentiated by the type of data they hold. In more complex languages like C++ or Java, variables are *typed* according to the type of data they hold. In Python, declaring and initializing a variable is this simple:

```
blogName = "Edukwest"
```

Here, we've created a variable called **blogName** and initialized it with the string value "Edukwest." The equals sign in this context is the assignment operator. The string value "Edukwest" is being assigned to the variable **blogName**. There are actually three types of primary values we can store in variables.

Key in the following code. (Feel free to substitute your own values for the variables.)

> Comments are indicated by "#"

```
gpa = 3.82        #floating point number
age = 40          #integer
name = "Mark Lassoff"    #string
```

```
print name, "is ", age , " years old and had a
GPA much lower than ", gpa
```

Save your file as variables.py and run it with the Python command. Your output should appear similar to *figure 3.1*:

Figure 3.1: Variables.py executing in the Koding.com virtual Linux environment.

I used comments to indicate the types of variables that were being created. Regardless of the type of variable being created, the syntax is the same. To review, the types of variables are:

 String: String variables are comprised of a series of characters in a particular order that have no mathematical value.

 Integer: Integer variables contain whole number values with no decimal point.

 Floating Point Values: Floating point variables contain more precise numbers that have a whole number and fractional amount represented by a decimal point value.

Variables are dynamic, in that the value can be changed or reassigned through the life of the program. Imagine, for example, that in a video game you have a variable that tracks the player's score. As the player's score changes, that value would go up until the game is over. Once the game ends, the value inside the player's score variable might be reassigned the value zero.

Consider the following code:

```
first = raw_input("What is your first name? ")
last  = raw_input("What is your last name? ")
fullName= first + " " + last
print fullName
middle = raw_input("What is your middle name? ")
fullName = first + " "  + middle + " " + last
print fullName
```

Entering the code and running the program yields the following result:

Figure 3.2: During the lifetime of the fullName variable, the value is reassigned

Note that when we first declare the **fullName** variable, it is assigned the values of **first** and **last** concatenated by the + sign. That value is then printed to the console. As the program continues to execute, the value of **fullName** is reassigned to include the variable **middle** as well. When a variable is assigned a new value, its original value is cleared and replaced with the new value.

ARITHMETIC WITH VARIABLES

Variables are frequently used as part of arithmetic expressions in Python. Arithmetic in Python is no different than the arithmetic you learned in grade school. The following symbols are used:

+	Addition
-	Subtraction
*	Multiplication
/	Division
%	Modulus

If you are new to programming, modulus may be unfamiliar to you, but the concept is easy—modulus is the remainder after division. For example:

10 % 3 = 1
11 % 3 = 2
12 % 3 = 0

> **Talk the Talk:**
> *Most programmers will say 'mod' for short when they are talking about modulus.*

I frequently use modulus when programming in order to determine if a number is even or odd. Any even number used with modulus 2 will result in zero.

Math with variables looks pretty much as you'd expect. Key in the following example program:

```
operand1 = 3432.4
operand2 = 1232.55

print operand1 + operand2
print operand1 - operand2
print operand1 * operand2
print operand1 / operand2
print 14 % 5
```

In this program two variables are declared as operand1 and operand2. Then the operands are put in two expressions using addition, subtraction, multiplication, and division. A final print statement uses the modulus statement in an expression. When you run the program with the python command, the result should appear similar to this:

```
Marks-MacBook-Pro-3:PythonExamples marklassoff$ vi math.py
Marks-MacBook-Pro-3:PythonExamples marklassoff$ python math.py
4664.95
2199.85
4230604.62
2.78479574865
4
Marks-MacBook-Pro-3:PythonExamples marklassoff$
```

Figure 3.3: Python program evaluating several mathematical expressions and outputting the result to the console.

When working with arithmetic in programming, it's important to keep in mind the order of operations. Let's use Python's interactive mode for this example. At your system prompt, just type **Python**. This will put you in Python's interactive mode where you can interact with the Python interpreter directly. Using the next example as your guide, enter the following and see if you can explain the result in terms of the order of operations.

```
Marks-MacBook-Pro-3:PythonExamples marklassoff$ python
Python 2.7.5 (default, Aug 25 2013, 00:04:04)
[GCC 4.2.1 Compatible Apple LLVM 5.0 (clang-500.0.68)] on darwin
Type "help", "copyright", "credits" or "license" for more information.
>>> 2+2
4
>>> 2*2+2
6
>>> 2+2*2
6
>>> 2+2*3
8
>>> (2+2)*3
12
>>> 2/9+2
2
>>> 2+9/2
6
>>> (2+9)/2
5
>>>
```

Figure 3.4: Different expressions are evaluated in Python's interactive mode demonstrating the order of operations.

Was the result always what you expected? The order of operations determines what part of a mathematical expression is evaluated first. Expressions are evaluated from left to right generally, but the specific order of operations is:

1) Parenthesis
2) Exponents
3) Multiplication
4) Division
5) Addition
6) Subtraction

A common error made by new programmers is to incorrectly interpret the order of operations within a math-related problem. When this happens, a program will still run, but will often give an incorrect result.

WORKING WITH STRINGS

Python is frequently used to manipulate strings. In fact, manipulating strings is a common task for programmers. Imagine, for example, you're given a list of data where first and last names are combined into a single field. Using string manipulation techniques, you'd have to separate them into fields by extracting data from the string.

The different **Python String Methods** will allow you to manipulate strings in every way imaginable. You can see the Python documentation on the String Methods here: https://docs.python.org/release/2.5.2/lib/string-methods.html.

Let's work with a few String Methods. Key in the following program. This program demonstrates just a few of the string functions. You don't have to type the embedded comments if you don't want to, they are just for your reference.

```python
phrase = "The quick brown fox jumped over the lazy dogs."
print len(phrase)  #length of the phrase in characters
print phrase.index("fox")   #Where is fox in the phrase
print phrase.replace("jumped", "galavanted") #replace jumped with new word
print phrase.swapcase()  #Swap upper and lower
```

Once you run the program, you should see a result similar to *figure 3.5*:

Figure 3.5: String manipulation result in Python

As you can see, Python's string manipulation features are powerful.

CHAPTER 4

CONDITIONALS AND LOOPS

In the last chapter we took a close look at variables. In this chapter, we're going to be using variables again. First, we'll be using variables to make decisions and execute branching within our program. Then we'll use variables to create loops that iterate through a portion of code a number of times. Conditionals and loops, the two concepts that we have covered up to now, are found in just about every programming language. So far, the programs we've written are all serial—they go through the same steps in the same order each time. With the addition of conditionals and loops to our programming repertoire, your programs will be able to vary their path based on conditions you set. Sounds like fun, right?

SIMPLE CONDITIONALS

Let's start by entering some code. Fire up your development environment and enter the following code using nano or vi:

```
age = input("How old are you: ")
if age >= 21:
        print "You are legally able to drink"
```

When you've entered the program in your text editor, run it three separate times. The first time, enter an age older than 21. The next time you run it, enter an age younger than 21. When you run it one final time, enter 21 exactly. To make sure the program runs correctly we want to test all the possible scenarios for execution.

Your output should appear similar to *figure 4.1*:

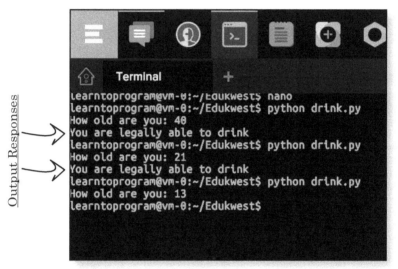

Output Responses

Figure 4.1: Program being tested for three different types of user responses.

This three-line program is pretty straightforward. What's new is the *if* statement. In this case we're determining if the value the user entered is *greater than or equal to* 21. The portion of the if statement written like this: age>=21 is known as the *condition*. Every conditional statement has a condition that is evaluate to be *true* or *false*. If it's true, the code indented underneath the conditional statement is executed.

if statement

Note in the example shown in *figure 4.1*, the program responds "You are legally able to drink" only if the user enters a value 21 or greater. If the code block that runs if the condition is true extends more than one line, please note that each line must have the same level of indentation below the conditional statement.

Python is a bit unusual for modern languages in that it uses indentation to demarcate code blocks. More traditionally, brackets are used to contain blocks of code.

WHAT ELSE?

You probably noted that the program we wrote responds only if the conditional is evaluated as true. If the conditional is evaluated as false, the user receives no response. This is likely confusing for the user. We're going to add to the program so that it reacts one way if the condition is evaluated as true and another way if the condition is evaluated as false.

```python
age = input("How old are you: ")
if age >= 21:
        print "You are legally able to drink"
else:
        print "You are not of drinking age."
```

After modifying your program code, run through the three possible scenarios as you did before. Test a case where the user is under 21, another where the user is older than 21, and a final scenario where the user is exactly 21. Your output should appear similar to *figure 4.2*:

Figure 4.2 Result with the else statement added.

As you can tell, the addition of the *else* statement gave a result if a value under 21 was entered. When the user enters a value under 21, the condition is evaluated as false and the else statement block is triggered. Once again, the level of indentation determines what code is in the statement block.

else statement

Let's add just a little bit more code to our program:

```
age = input("How old are you: ")
if age >= 21:
        print "You are legally able to drink"
else:
        print "You are not of drinking age."
if age == 21:
        print "Congratulations, here's a free
drink."
```

Now, if the user says they are exactly 21, the program will print the congratulatory message. Note that the comparison operator == was used to denote equality. If the value in age is exactly 21, the conditional is evaluated as true.

Here are all the comparison operators that you can use with *if* statements:

IF STATEMENT COMPARISON OPERATORS	
==	Equal
>	Greater Than
>=	Greater Than or Equal
<	Less Than
<=	Less Than or Equal
!=	Not Equal

While you can already see the power of conditionals, let's add a layer of complexity: what if you wanted to test two values at once?

COMPOUND CONDITIONALS

Let's pretend that we're writing software for a college to determine whether or not a specific student made the honor roll. In our college, in order to be eligible for honors you must both have a GPA greater than 3.5 and attempt more than 12 hours.

Create a new program in your text editor called honors.py and enter the code below in the file:

```python
gpa = input("What is your GPA this semester? "
)
hours = input("How many credit hours did you
attempt? ")

if gpa > 3.5 and hours > 12:
        print "Congratulations, You are on the
honor roll"
else:
        print "Sorry.  You did not make honor
roll.  Better luck next time."
```

Test your program and see what kind of result you get. Your result should be similar to what appears in *figure 4.3*:

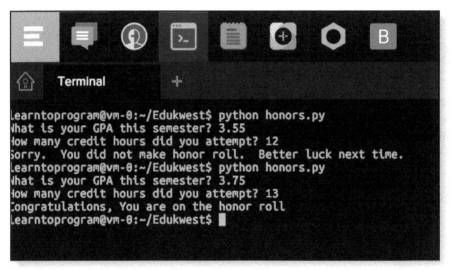

Figure 4.3: Two conditions are tested simultaneously.

You'll notice that in the **if** statement we joined two conditions by the word **and**, which, in this case, is acting as an operator. In this if statement both conditions joined by *and* must be evaluated as true in order for the whole statement to be true. The **or** operator can be used in other circumstances where one condition or the other must be true. You can join any amount of conditions in a single if statement with **and** and **or** operators.

```
gpa = input("What is your GPA this semester? " )
hours = input("How many credit hours did you
attempt? ")

if gpa > 3.5 and hours > 12:
        print "Congratulations, You are on the
honor roll"
else:
        print "Sorry.  You did not make honor
roll.  Better luck next time."
```

and **operators**   *or* **operators**

COMPLEX CONDITIONALS WITH ELIF

So far the conditionals we've created can make decisions in an either/ or scenario—either you are eligible to drink, or you're not. However, life is more complex than this, which is why if statements can be paired with *elif* (else-if) statements. This combination will let you choose from several options as in the program below.

elif statement

Please key in this program and run it with the Python command to see the result:

```python
age = input("Enter your age: ")

if age < 18:
        print "You're a kid!"
        print "Go to school."
elif age < 29:
        print "It's time to be establishing
yourself in life"
        print "Good luck"
elif age < 39:
        print "These are good years to focus on
career"
        print "Get a job"
elif age < 49:
        print "Time to start thinking about
retirement"
        print "I hope you are putting money
away"
elif age < 59:
        print "Maintain your health through
exercise"
        print "Get a trainer"
else:
        print "You are old"
```

With apologies to those 59 and older, this program provides feedback based on the age the user enters. First the user enters their age and this value is assigned to the variable *age*. The value entered by the user is then tested in the first part of the if statement. If the age is less than 18, the program responds with "You're a kid! Go to school."

If the first condition turns out to be false, the *elif* condition is evaluated. If the age is less than 29, the appropriate advice is dispensed. If not, the next statement is evaluated. If none of the conditions associated with the *elif* statements are found to be true, then the unfortunate *else* statement at the end of the program runs.

Keep in mind that *elif* statements are only run if all of the previous conditions are found to be false. Note also the indentation used throughout the *else/elif/else* is consistent, as is required in the Python programming language.

WHILE LOOPS

Loops allow you to run a block of code a number of times. Each time that block of code is executed is known as an *iteration*. Loops are critical to many different types of programs. Imagine a card game where turns are taken and cards are dealt—all with loops. If you think about it, you can probably identify loops in many different types of software that you use every day.

loops

The process of waiting for the user to input something, processing that input and then waiting for the user again is often coded in a loop structure.

Run the program with the Python command and the result should appear something like what you see in *figure 4.4*:

Let's code a simple loop:

```
x = 0
while x < 100:
        print x
        x += 5
print "EOE"
```

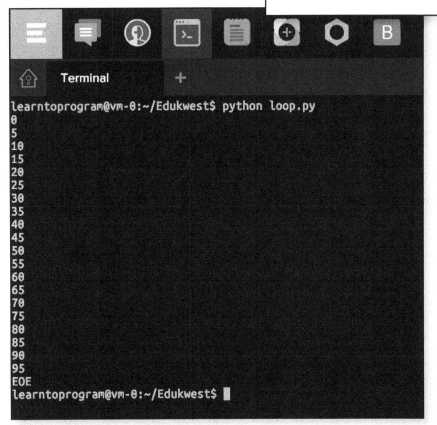

```
learntoprogram@vm-0:~/Edukwest$ python loop.py
0
5
10
15
20
25
30
35
40
45
50
55
60
65
70
75
80
85
90
95
EOE
learntoprogram@vm-0:~/Edukwest$
```

Figure 4.4: The result of a while loop.

In the first line of this program we initialize a variable *x* at the value 0. Next comes our *while* statement which states that while the value of *x* is less than 100, the code block indented below the *while* statement will execute. In this case, **while statement** the code block prints the value of *x* to the console and then increases the value *x* by 5. Note that the x+=5 notation is shorthand for x=x+5. += is known as a combined assignment operator.

Here's another loop example program for you to try. I saved mine as loop2.py.

```python
band = ""
while band != "XXX":
        band = raw_input("Name a band you like
or XXX to stop: ")
        if band != "XXX":
                print band, "ROCKS!"
```

Run the program with the Python command and you should see a result similar to *figure 4.5*:

Figure 4.5 The user inputs text inside a loop.

When this program initially runs, the variable *band* is set to an empty string. The value of *band* is compared to the string "XXX" each time through the loop. If the loop is anything other than "XXX" the loop iterates again. If the value is not XXX, the name of the band is echoed back to the console. Once again, notice the indentation in the source code.

DON'T TRY THIS AT HOME

A common error in programming is an endless loop. An endless loop is a loop that never ends. These endless loops can consume more and more computing resources and eventually make the program crash—or worse.

You'll note that the continuation condition will **always** be true in this example—the value of *x* will always be greater than zero. The value of *x* very rapidly gets out of hand and, in fact, becomes too big to store in memory. I ran this in the Koding.com environment and also peeked at the resources being used by my Mac at the time.

CONSIDER THE FOLLOWING CODE:

```
x = 1
while x > 0:
        print x
        x *= 2
```

Figure 4.6: At this point the browser was frozen, but Google Chrome and associated threads took up more than their share of CPU resources.

You can try this example on your own. I'm not responsible for any damage done. (Damage won't be permanent...have fun!)

CHAPTER 5

DEALING WITH DATA

In the last chapter we examined control structures, conditionals, and loops, which are critical in most programming languages. They allow your programs to make decisions based on the criteria that you set as the developer. In this chapter, we're going to switch gears and examine data and how it's stored. We'll take a close look at three data structures: lists, tuples, and dictionaries. You may not have given much thought to data before. The easiest way to conceptualize data is as organized information.

Different types of information lend themselves to being organized in different ways. For example, if your data is a grocery list, then a list would be the optimal way to organize your data. However, if you wanted to store student grades on different assignments over a period of time, a list wouldn't work well at all. There are many different data structures used by programmers and each is optimized for a different type of data.

Let's start with a simple grocery list.

LISTS

 We've all made a grocery list before, but you likely haven't stored it in Python code. Let's do that now using the following line of code:

```
groceries = [ "apples" , "potatoes" , "bread" ,
"milk" , "butter", "oranges", "salt" , "sugar"
, "cereal" ]
```

Unlike variables, which store a single unit of data, we've stored multiple elements in our list. I'm sure you can imagine a number of situations where this could be convenient. In this case, all of the *members* of our list are strings. You might also create a list using floating point numbers, integers, or some combination of both. Here is a list of floating point values:

members

```
gpas = [ 3.25, 2.26, 1.99, 3.55, 4.0, 3.21,
2.56, 3.06 , 2.72 ]
```

Now, here's where it gets more interesting. Because lists are considered objects in the Python programming language, there are a number of build-in commands that you can use to work with lists. This is actually a really big deal because there are included functions that do things like count the members of the list or sort them. You could do this with your own Python code, but trust me, it would be a lot of work.

*Note: We'll talk more about **objects** in the next chapter, so if this concept is confusing, don't worry.*

Before we get into the really fancy stuff, let's take a look at how we extract data from the list. Key in the two lists above, along with a few additional lines of code.

```
groceries = [ "apples" , "potatoes" , "bread" ,
"milk" , "butter", "oranges", "salt" , "sugar"
, "cereal" ]
gpas = [ 3.25, 2.26, 1.99, 3.55, 4.0, 3.21,
2.56, 3.06 , 2.72 ]
print groceries[0]
print groceries[4]
print gpas[3]
```

Once you're sure that the code is typed correctly in your text editor, execute the code with the **Python** command. Your output should look like this:

Pay special attention to the print statements. You'll note that each print statement references one of our lists and a specific index within that list surrounded by brackets. Lists in Python, like most languages, are indexed, meaning that each member of the list is assigned a number used to reference it. The first member of a list is always index zero.

index

Our grocery list would have the following indexes:

When combined with the **print** command, the general form of retrieving data from a list is:

```
print
listname[index]
```

Index	Member
0	apples
1	potatoes
2	break
3	milk
4	butter
5	oranges
6	salt
7	sugar
8	cereal

If you've worked with other programming languages, you may think that lists are very similar to the concept of arrays. You're correct!

One thing to keep in mind is that your list is only as long as you make it. If you try to access a non-existent list index, your program is going to exit with an error. Let's add one line to our current program:

```
print gpas[17]
```

When you run the program you should see an output similar to the following:

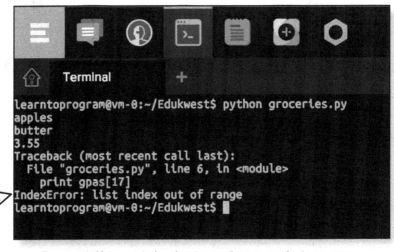

Figure 5.2: Using an index that is out of range results in an error.

EDITING LIST MEMBERS

You can also use the index of a list member to change the values of
different members in the list. This is done with an assignment statement
as in assigning a value to a standard variable. The following statement
will change the zeroth index of the GPA list:

```
gpas[0] = 4.0
```

Note that the indexes of the other members of the lists are not affected.

USING LIST FUNCTIONS

Earlier I mentioned that lists are objects, which allows you to use a
number of functions associated with the list object. You might want to
take a look at the official Python documentation and see the functions
that you can use with lists.

The documentation is available at
https://docs.python.org/2/tutorial/datastructures.html.

Let's add two more lines of code to demonstrate the use of the **append()**
function.

append()

```
groceries.append("chicken")
print groceries
```

We use the **append()** function with the dot notation and associate it with
the list name. In this case, we're adding "chicken" in the first available
index of the groceries list. The length of the list is effectively expanded
with the use of the **append()** function.

Once you add the new code to your program, run the program in your browser. You should see an output similar to figure 5.3:

Figure 5.3: Note that when output with the print command, 'chicken' appears at the end of the groceries list.

Let's try one more list function. The **sort()** function does exactly what it sounds like—it sorts the members of the list. Its usage is similar to usage of the append function. Add the following two lines of code to your program:

sort()

```
groceries.sort()
print "Sorted: ", groceries
```

Run your program with the Python command. Your output should look something like this:

Figure 5.4: After the **sort()** function runs, the groceries list is reindexed. Apples is now in the zeroth index, potatoes in the first index, and so on.

TUPLES

Tuples are very similar to lists with one important exception: tuples are non-dynamic. Once a tuple is defined, the values within it cannot be changed. Let's start a new program where we will define a tuple.

```
widths = (600, 800, 1024, 1280, 1366, 1920)
print widths
print widths[2]
widths[0] = 500
```

Run the code using the Python command and carefully examine the output.

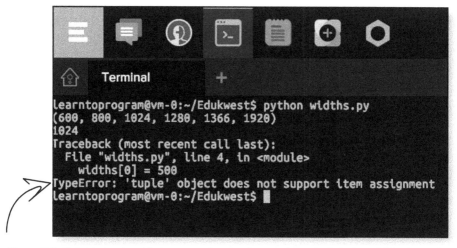

Figure 5.5: Note that we're able to access the complete tuple, a single index within the tuple, but when reassigning a value within a tuple, an error is generated. A tuple is non-dynamic and once initiated, the values within it cannot be changed.

Tuples are for storing data that does not change over the life of a program. For example, in the program above, the screen widths are unlikely to change.

DICTIONARIES

Dictionaries are another data structure. Dictionaries are perfect for storing paired data, sometimes known as *key: value* data. In this type of data instead of a numerical index, each data point is indexed by a key which is determined by the programmer. State names and state capitals or towns and zip codes are both examples of where dictionaries can be useful to store data.

key

value

Consider the following program:

```python
states = {        'Connecticut' : 'Hartford',
                  'New York': 'Albany',
                  'Mississippi': 'Jackson',
                  'Maine': 'Augusta',
                  'Montana': 'Helena',
                  'Texas': 'Austin' }

print states['Maine']
```

When you run the program with the Python command you'll see the output "Augusta." Essentially, the key (or index) for "Augusta" is "Maine." Note the print command and how it is used to access the value in the dictionary.

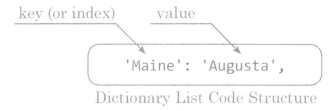

key (or index)   value

'Maine': 'Augusta',

Dictionary List Code Structure

Just like lists, Python dictionaries are an object and have functions that can be associated with them. Let's take a look at one of these functions.

Update your code so it looks like this:

```
states = {          'Connecticut' : 'Hartford',
                    'New York': 'Albany',
                    'Mississippi': 'Jackson',
                    'Maine': 'Augusta',
                    'Montana': 'Helena',
                    'Texas': 'Austin' }

print states
print "Values:" , states.values()
print "Keys:", states.keys()
```

Run your code on the command line using the Python command. Your result should appear similar to figure 5.6:

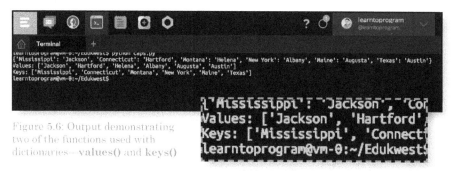

Figure 5.6: Output demonstrating two of the functions used with dictionaries—**values()** and **keys()**

You'll note that the **values()** function returns all of the values in the dictionary, while the **keys()** function returns all of the keys.

This short chapter can only give you a broad introduction to working with data in programming. Almost every program, to some degree, works with data. Being effective at working with data is an important part of any programmer's toolbox.

CHAPTER 6

PUTTING IT ALL TOGETHER

Classes and objects represent not just a programming concept, but a way of looking at the world and solving problems. Classes and objects, at a high level, represent a process of classification—an activity that is as old as science. When we create a class, we create a model of an object that breaks the object down to its core activities and attributes. While the Python programming language supports classes and objects, some languages, like Java, are completely dependent on them. The reason to learn them now is because classes and objects are critical in working with many modern-day programming languages.

CLASS VERSUS OBJECTS

I often tell my students to think of a class as a blueprint of an object. From that blueprint many instances of the class (objects) can be created. Think of planned housing communities: a single blueprint, may be used to build many different homes. These homes may vary in substantial ways—they may be different colors, have different kitchen counters, and different fixtures in the bathrooms—but they are all still based on the same blueprint.

class

object

In programming, a class defines how an object of the class is described and what it can do. I often tell my classroom students to think of classes as a set of adjectives and a set of verbs. The adjectives give us a way to describe the class, while the verbs tell us what the class can do. The set of adjectives used to describe a class are known as **properties**. The set of verbs associated with a class are known as **methods**.

If we were describing a class "vehicle" we might include the following methods and properties:

Properties (Adjectives)	Methods (verbs)
color	accelerate()
weight	decelerate()

height	turnLeft()
topSpeed	turnRight()
vehicleType	startIngnition()
	stopIgnition()

Obviously this model is greatly simplified. If we were truly trying to represent a vehicle in code, we'd likely have to use several interrelated classes. In languages other than Python we'd also have to declare the type of data each property would hold. For example, the color property would hold a string, while weight, height, and top speed could be integers. When we create an instance of the Vehicle Class that we defined in the previous table, we might assign a value to all of the properties, like this:

```
theVehicle.color = "blue"
theVehicle.weight = 5565
theVehicle.height = 48
theVehicle.topSpeed = 90
theVehicle.vehicleType = "car"
```

This example assumes an instance (object) created called theVehicle.

CODING A CLASS IN PYTHON

Let's write the code that represents an Animal class in Python. We'll also create an instance of that class called myDog.

```
class Animal:

        numAnimals = 0

        def __init__(self, length, weight,
color, presenceOfFur):
                self.length = length
                self.weight = weight
                self.color = color
                self.presenceOfFur =
presenceOfFur
                Animal.numAnimals += 1

myDog = Animal(19, 12, "brown", "true")

print myDog.length
```

There are definitely a few new things here. We start our definition of the class with the **class** keyword and then the name of the class—in this case, "Animal." Next, you'll notice I declare a variable called **numAnimals** and initialize it at zero. The numAnimals variable is simply designed to do some internal housekeeping in the class. Its job, specifically, is to track how many instances of Animal we create.

We then define with the **def** keyword a function called **__init__**. This function runs every time a new instance of Animal is created. Passed into this function are the values for the length, weight, and other properties of the Animal instance. You can see these values being passed into the __init__ function in this line of code:

def

```
myDog = Animal(19, 12, "brown", "true")
```

The particular instance of Animal that we are creating, called **myDog,** has a length of 19, weight of 12, is brown, and has fur. The first four lines of the __init__ function assign these values that are passed into the instance.

```
Marks-MacBook-Pro-3:PythonExamples marklassoff$ nano Animal.py

  GNU nano 2.0.6              File: Animal.py

class Animal:

        numAnimals = 0

        def __init__(self, length, weight, color, presenceOfFur):
                self.length = length
                self.weight = weight
                self.color = color
                self.presenceOfFur = presenceOfFur
                Animal.numAnimals += 1

myDog = Animal(19, 12, "brown", "true")

print myDog.length
```

Figure 6.1: Creating the class in nano

Examine the following line:

```
Animal.numAnimals += 1
```

This line is designed to increment the value of numAnimals, the internal housekeeping variable that keeps track of how many instances of Animal we generate. The actual instance is generated with the next line of code. The final line of code accesses the length property of the myDog instance of Animal and displays it.

ADDING SOME METHODS

Let's change up and add to our initial code:

```
class Animal:

        numAnimals = 0

        def __init__(self, length, weight,
color, presenceOfFur, hungry):
                self.length = length
                self.weight = weight
                self.color = color
                self.presenceOfFur =
presenceOfFur
                self.hungry = hungry
                Animal.numAnimals += 1

        def walk(self):
                print "Animal is walking"

        def eat(self):
                self.hungry = "false"
                print "Animal is eating"
                self.weight  += .1

myDog = Animal(19, 12, "brown", "true", "true")
myDog.walk()
myDog.eat()
print myDog.length
```

When you run the code with the Python command in your command line, the result should look something like this:

```
Marks-MacBook-Pro-3:PythonExamples marklassoff$ python Animal.py
Animal is walking
Animal is eating
Animal now weighs  12.1
19
Marks-MacBook-Pro-3:PythonExamples marklassoff$
```

Figure 6.2: Creating an instance of a class and manipulating it

You'll notice that I've added an additional property to the class: hungry. This property is designed simply to track whether or not the instance of Animal is hungry. When we create the instance of Animal called myDog, we set the value of the hungry property to true.

We've also added two methods to our class. The first method, walk(), simply prints out the message "Animal is walking."

The second method, eat(), is more complex. It interacts with the properties of the object. First, the eat() method sets the value of the hungry property to "false." It then informs the user that the Animal is eating via the print statement. Finally, because the animal is eating, we access the weight property and add .1 to its value.

After the class definition and the instantiation (fancy word for creation) of the myDog instance, we run the walk() and eat() methods.

MULTIPLE INSTANCES

You'll remember from our initial discussion that a class is merely a
blueprint and multiple objects can be constructed from that class. Enter
this revised code in your text editor:

```
class Animal:

        numAnimals = 0

        def __init__(self,name, length, weight,
color, presenceOfFur, hungry):
                self.name = name
                self.length = length
                self.weight = weight
                self.color = color
                self.presenceOfFur =
presenceOfFur
                self.hungry = hungry
                Animal.numAnimals += 1

        def walk(self):
                print self.name, " is walking"

        def eat(self):
                self.hungry = "false"
                print self.name ,  " is eating"

myDog = Animal("Rover",19, 12, "brown", "true",
"true")
myDog.walk()
myDog.eat()
print myDog.length

yourDog = Animal("Murray", 15,14, "black",
"true", "true")
yourDog.walk()
yourDog.eat()
```

I've added yet another property to the Animal class. The name property is designed to hold the name of the Animal instance. Keep in mind, this is distinct from the name of the code reference to the instance. In the previous code, the original Animal instance myDog has a value of "Rover" in the name property, while the new object has a value of "Murray" in the name property.

```
Marks-MacBook-Pro-3:PythonExamples marklassoff$ python Animal.py
Rover   is walking
Rover   is eating
Rover   now weighs   12.1
19
Murray  is walking
Murray  is eating
Murray  now weighs   14.1
Marks-MacBook-Pro-3:PythonExamples marklassoff$
```

Figure 6.3: Two instances of Animal objects are created—Rover and Murray.

This section was designed to give you only a basic introduction to object-oriented programming with classes and objects. However, you will find that these foundational concepts can be applied to many modern programming languages.

The end of this section also brings us to the conclusion of this book. You now know the foundations of programming using the Python programming language. You will find this information useful whether you continue your study in Python, or move to other areas of development, such as web applications or mobile.

Whatever direction you go, I wish you the best of luck.

www.ingramcontent.com/pod-product-compliance
Lightning Source LLC
Chambersburg PA
CBHW061034050326
40689CB00012B/2819